God's goal is for us

to become mature

adults – to be fully

grown, measured by

the standard of

the fullness of Christ.

Ephesians 4:13 (CEB)

Ken Willard has poured years of ministry leadership experience into the pages of this resource, which is filled with adaptable and customizable concepts for churches of any size, setting, and circumstance. Significantly, the emphasis of the book upon the non-negotiable role of ongoing prayer to fuel congregations as they identify their core values provides what's foundationally needed to jumpstart an exciting next season.

Sue Nilson Kibbey
Director, Bishop Bruce Ough Innovation Center

In these pages, your church leaders are invited to quality time with a seasoned ministry development guide. Ken Willard has walked with hundreds of churches down the road of helping them clarify what on earth they are seeking to do and why they care enough to do it. The longer your church has been around, the more likely you are flying on autopilot and steadily losing altitude. Ken Willard can help your church soar again.

Paul Nixon
Author, *Cultural Competency;* Co-Author, *Launching a New Worship Community*

Core values are operative in every organization, whether or not time is taken to name those values. Ken Willard lays out a simple yet powerfully effective process for making the invisible known. All churches can benefit from this review of *Identifying Core Values.*

Jaye Johnson
Dir. of Congregational Excellence, Iowa Conference of the UMC

Ken Willard's *Identifying Core Values* offers an extraordinarily insightful and practical guide to all Jesus Christ followers, the Christian church, and its current and future leaders. All leaders, members, and participants in the mission and ministry of Christ's church who genuinely strive to discover who God is calling them to be and find consistency, accountability, and guidance for living into and staying on track in their Christian identity. I believe every leader will greatly benefit from Willard's prayerful, biblical and systematic process to Identify Core Values.

James L. Friday
Dir. of Congregational Excellence, South Carolina Conference of the UMC

These little books in *The Greatest Expedition* series are gifts to the church, just as Ken is. In this piece, he guides churches through a step-by-step process of establishing core values, which he also calls a boundary for the church. What a helpful metaphor for values. Easy to read, accessible, and practical. It's what many leaders are looking for in these hectic times. A great resource!

Derrek Belase
Executive Dir. of Connectional Ministry, Oklahoma Conference of the UMC

As a church planter, pastor, and now developer, I frequently refer to the core values of the organization I lead to guide my teams, especially when difficult conversations become necessary. In *Identifying Core Values of the New Expedition,* Ken Willard offers a timely, practical, and accessible resource for an organization to identify and develop its core values and understand how an organization lives into these values. In this season of great change, now is a crucial time for cime as this!

Owen Ross
Dir. of Church Development, North Texas Conference of the UMC

Ken Willard has given us a gift: a step-by-step tool for any church needing to discern values that can guide their decisions as they make disciples of Jesus Christ on their journey of *The Greatest Expedition.* I highly recommend this book if you wonder how you go about discerning your local church's values and then living out those unique values in your unique mission field!

Gloria Fowler
Dir. of Congregational Dev. and Transformation, Louisiana Conference of the UMC

There are seasons in the life of every church when, for various reasons, church leadership feels as if the church is stuck. The church may be "stuck" because it uses all of its resources on a plethora of ministries that lack purpose or direction. It may be stuck because key informal leaders are resistant to creative ministry opportunities. The church may be stuck because there is a lack of clarity about a new way of being to which the church is being called. Ken Willard has offered practical, easily implemented tools for church leaders to guide their congregation in a spiritual process to clarify purpose, values, and direction so that the congregation might move forward with a well-defined vision and mission. The process Willard outlines can be used in a variety of contexts to garner support and shared ownership of ministry and mission throughout a faith community. I commend this book to all who may feel stuck or moving and want to ensure they are moving in God's direction.

Bishop Cynthia Moore-Koikoi
Western Pennsylvania Conference of the UMC

IDENTIFYING
Core
Values

of the New Expedition

Ken Willard

the greatest
EXPEDITION

IDENTIFYING
Core
Values
of the New Expedition

books@marketsquarebooks.com
141 N. Martinwood Rd. Knoxville TN 37923
ISBN: 978-1-950899-45-6

Printed and Bound in the United States of America
Cover Illustration & Book Design ©2021 Market Square Publishing, LLC

Contributing Editor: Kay Kotan

**Unless noted, Scripture quotations taken from
the CEB version of the Holy Bible:**

CEB

NIV

This resource was commissioned as
one of many interconnected steps in the
journey of *The Greatest Expedition*.

GreatestExpedition.com

Table of Contents

Foreword

This resource was commissioned as one of many interconnected steps in the journey of *The Greatest Expedition*. While each step is important individually, we intentionally built the multi-step Essentials Pack and the Expansion Pack to provide a richer and fuller experience with the greatest potential for transformation and introducing more people to a relationship with Jesus Christ. For more information, visit GreatestExpedition.org.

However, we also recognize you may be exploring this resource apart from *The Greatest Expedition*. You might find yourself on a personal journey, a small group journey, or perhaps a church leadership team journey. We are so glad you are on this journey!

As you take each step in your expedition,

your Expedition Team will discover whether the ministry tools you will be exploring will be utilized only for the Expedition Team or if this expedition will be a congregational journey. Our hope and prayer is *The Greatest Expedition* is indeed a congregational journey, but if it proves to be a solo journey for just the Expedition Team, God will still do amazing things through your intentional exploration, discernment, and faithful next steps.

Regardless of how you came to discover *The Greatest Expedition,* it will pave the way to a new God-inspired expedition. Be brave and courageous on your journey through *The Greatest Expedition!*

Kay L Kotan, PCC
Director, *The Greatest Expedition*

INTRODUCTION
Core Values

All churches have core values.

That is a theme you will hear several times throughout this book. Your ministry, no matter how old or how new, is operating now with a set of values. Our role as leaders in the church is to invest the time and energy to identify those values and to use them wisely as we make ministry decisions and guide us toward God's vision.

In August of 2021, Bonnie MacDonald and I traveled to an installation service for a District Superintendent in our Conference. We drove there in her Subaru Outback. Several times on the winding highway roads the vehicle would go over a line on the road and an audible sound would alert us thanks to the "Lane Departure and Sway Warning" system.

While that warning beep might be a nuance in situations where it is practically unavoidable to stay between the lines at all times due to the sharp curves in the road, I can see where it would be very helpful to most drivers.

As you read through this book about core values, I would challenge you to begin thinking about a time when you and your leadership team have discerned the core values of your ministry. What type of "warning" system would help you to stay on track? What could you possibly put in place to let you know when your ministry is "going over the line" in relation to your values? Those are not questions you will likely be able to answer now, but they will become very important to you very soon.

On the trip back from the installation service there was such heavy rain that the vehicle flashed a warning many times that the "Lane Departure and Sway Warning" was currently inoperable. Apparently, the rain was so hard that it covered the cameras.

Even with a system in place to let you know when you are straying beyond one or more of your core values, you will likely face storms in your ministry which could put those systems at risk. The core values you discern for your ministry are too important for you to let anything distract you or force you to cross over the line.

While it is true that all churches have core values, my guess would be that very few of them have ever gone through a process of intentional discernment to identify those values. Having this book in your hands means that you are going where few ministry leaders have gone before. This journey is too important for you to take it on your own.

Some of you may be making this trip with your Expedition Team. That is wonderful. For those of you reading this who are not taking part in The Greatest Expedition, I would encourage you now to prayerfully invite a few other key leaders in your ministry to join you on the journey. Get them a copy of this book and read it together. You will then have a few other people to process the learning, create a plan, and hold each other accountable.

There is an old saying I have been fond

of using for many years. "Information + Application = Transformation." In today's church world that is not enough. Now I feel that it needs to be, "Information + Application + Accountability = Transformation. The work God is calling us to accomplish in this season of ministry is too important for us to not have positive, Christian accountability built in at all stages.

May God's Spirit guide you and your team on this journey of discovery!

CHAPTER ONE
What Do I Pack?

*Core values are the positive,
predictable behavior patterns church
members expect of each other in daily
routines and daring activities.*

Thomas G. Bandy, Strategic
Thinking: How to Sustain Effective Ministry

What do I pack for the trip?

That is a question most people have asked
at some point in their lives. If you are going
to a city, state, or country where you have
never traveled before, the focus might be on
bringing the appropriate types of clothing
for the climate. When persons who lives
in warmer climates travels to much colder
climates for the first time, they usually
learn the importance of dressing in layers.
Depending on your mode of transportation,

a person might also need to consider what to put in a bag they will check at the airport and what they want to keep with them on the flight. When you talk to a person who travels a lot, you will usually hear them share how they have learned to pack efficiently, only bringing with them the items they feel are most essential.

As you begin this new expedition journey, it is essential for you to, too, discern what matters most for you to hold close. What can guide you, support you, and keep you grounded on this expedition? Consider the image of a scout going away for a long hike with their troop. What will they pack into their backpack? Imagine a young scout at home the night before their first long hike. They spread on their bed all kinds of items they want to bring:

- A Swiss Army Knife
- Extra socks
- Comic books
- A Bible
- A jar of peanut butter

- A first aid kit

- A flashlight

- Tissues

- Skittles

- Electronic games

- A water bottle

- Gum

- Headphones

- Batteries

- A candy bar

- Popcorn

- Sunscreen

- An umbrella

The whole bed is covered! Not only will it not fit in their backpack, but it will also be too heavy for them to lift, much less carry on a hike. Taking everything will cause the hiker to be slower and tire more easily. So, they must prioritize their items and only bring what they need.

CHAPTER TWO
Preparation

As an Expedition Team, you will need to remember that your journey is unique in this new season. The Expedition Team is being called into something new and is likely still discerning something new. With that in mind, you may need to adapt (as repeatedly suggested throughout) the process for identifying core values.

Part of your journey as the Expedition Team is to discern not only *what* and *where* God is calling you, but the *how* of the journey is also in play. While it is hopeful that your current congregation (if your Expedition Team is a part of a current congregation) is supportive of the Expedition Team and the emerging new expedition, it is possible the congregation may simply be in a different place than the Expedition Team. The Expedition Team may discern in the core values process that the core values of the existing congregation have and continue to be holding back new expeditions God is calling us to reach. While we pray this is not the case, we also want to offer that it might be a possibility. Therefore, read the entire book before beginning the process. This will help you understand the process and why the process is vital to the Expedition Team's preparation for the new expedition. This will also provide a heads-up and open the conversation for the Expedition Team on whether the core values process is for the Expedition Team to use for the new and emerging expedition, or if the process indeed makes sense for a congregational approach since the expedition is undoubtedly a part of the larger ministry of the existing congregation. Knowing the process upfront will help the Expedition Team better understand the process, who should be involved, and focus the discernment.

CHAPTER THREE
Let's Get Started

Pause now and think about what you already know about core values. How would you define core values? You may not know much or anything about core values at this stage, which is fine. Hopefully, you will learn what you need in the following pages to take with you on this new expedition. If you have a good understanding of core values, then take a minute now to record some highlights of what you know on paper.

How would you explain core values to someone who has never heard of them before? You may also want to record any experiences with core values in the church or business worlds. Wherever you are now on your understanding of core values, prayerfully open your mind as you read the rest of this book to the possibility of hearing and learning something new from God's Spirit.

Core values are not only a part of what you will take with you on this new expedition. They can also help guide you on the journey and get you back on the right path if you get lost. Core values explain who we are – our identity. They explain why we do what we do. This is true for both organizations, like churches and individuals. In churches, the core values are the constant, passionate, biblical core beliefs that drive the ministry. Core values guide church leadership decisions and ministry direction.

As with all the areas of The Greatest Expedition, identifying your church's core values begins with prayer. Too often, organizational leaders – including those in local churches – will make the process of identifying core values an activity on the calendar. When leaders in the church lower core values to a task, it removes God from the process, and we end up listening only to ourselves and not the Holy Spirit.

Open your Bible to Acts 2 and read the very

familiar story of the Holy Spirit coming on the disciples at Pentecost. Now let's take a closer look at the end of that chapter. Picking up at verse 41:

> *Those who accepted Peter's message were baptized. God brought about three thousand people into the community on that day. The believers devoted themselves to the apostles' teaching, to the community, to their shared meals, and to their prayers. A sense of awe came over everyone. God performed many wonders and signs through the apostles. All the believers were united and shared everything. They would sell pieces of property and possessions and distribute the proceeds to everyone who needed them. Every day, they met together in the temple and ate in their homes. They shared food with gladness and simplicity. They praised God and demonstrated God's goodness to everyone. The Lord added daily to the community those who were being saved.*
>
> **Acts 2:41-47 (CEB)**

The early church had core values. However, it is doubtful they called them core values and equally unlikely identified as such in your Bible. The five essential core values of the Jerusalem church from our reading in the Book of Acts were:

1. **Evangelism** – we see this in verse 41 with "three thousand new people coming into the community" and verse 47 where "the Lord added daily to the community." Throughout the New Testament, we see evidence of this core value being passed along as new churches continued to reach new people for God.

2. **Instruction** – this core value is shown in verse 42, where we read that the "believers devoted themselves to the apostles' teaching." The Jewish tradition placed a strong emphasis on teaching and instruction. We see this throughout the Old Testament, and it is a core value the new church in Jerusalem brought with them.

3. **Fellowship** – is shown clearly in verse 42, where they "shared meals" and verses 44-46, where "the believers were united and shared everything." The value of fellowship is seen throughout the Bible. Look at how often stories and events are centered on meals or other types of gatherings. This value has been evidenced in churches for many years and continues to be important for all kinds of Christians today.

4. **Worship** – is clearly a core value in verses 42-43 and 46-47. The words in verse 47, "They praised God," certainly speak to the value of worship, and so do the other verses. Worship in the early church was not about style or music. It was about praising God. The believers in Jerusalem may have had to hide to avoid persecution, but they were still praising God.

5. **Service** – is a core value highlighted in verses 44-45, where we read about how the believers would "distribute the proceeds to everyone who needed them." The importance of giving to those in need, believers or not, is emphasized often throughout the Bible. The early church established this as a core value from the very beginning.

How will you intentionally make the identification of your church's core values a prayer-driven discernment process, and not a task to be checked off your "To-Do" list? There is, of course, no right or wrong way to include prayer and discernment in this process. You and your Expedition Team can and should come up with what works best for

> **In churches, the core values are the constant, passionate, biblical core beliefs that drive the ministry.**

your church. Making time to really listen to God is a key to any discernment. One way to do this is to prayer walk your community. Spending time in prayer as you stroll through the areas God is calling you to reach and serve is a great way to see things from God's perspective and listen for the whisper of the Holy Spirit. Gather a group, such as your Expedition Team, and start with a simple devotion, prayer, and some brief instructions. Keep in mind that many of us are used to talking to God, but most of us are not really practiced at listening to God. Listening for God's Spirit and observing what God is showing us are the keys to prayer walking.

Send people out to walk an area in pairs. This activity is not about drawing attention to ourselves, those in the community should have no idea what we are doing. The most important part of prayer walking is the debrief. This is the time you bring everyone back together and let them share what God showed them and what they heard whispered to them from the Holy Spirit. Through this time of sharing you should begin to hear trends or themes which will guide your work. There is a section on prayer walking in the book *Stride: Creating a Discipleship Pathway for Your Church* if you would like to learn more.

All churches have core values, and those core values drive the ministry of the church. However, most have never taken the time or effort to identify them. The question is not whether we have values, but which values go deep and truly guide our actions and decisions.

The core values of each church are unique. This is not just due to having different people in each church. There are many factors that tend to influence the values of a church. Think about your answers to each of these questions:

- What is our "founding story?" How did our church come into existence? If you are still living in this founding season, then identify the people and situations influencing your new ministry. The founding story of a church is very powerful.

This story can impact a ministry for generations, well beyond the lives of those personally involved. One small rural church was founded when a farmer sold two mules and donated the proceeds so the church could purchase land for their building. That value of generosity is still in place in that ministry today.

- What makes our church different from other churches? In some parts of the country, there is a church on every corner. This can be incredibly confusing to those unchurched people we are called to reach. We need to be very clear on the uniqueness of our ministry. A new church in the Midwest noticed that God kept sending them leaders in the community. A core value of leadership guided that church for years. They became known as a church that grew and developed leaders.

- What is it that attracts people to our church (or, in some cases, turns them away)? Why are you at this church? If you are the pastor and you were appointed to this church, then ask yourself, "Would you attend this church if you were not the pastor?" If so, then why? Think about these questions from the understanding that not everyone likes the same things everyone else does. The chances are good that even your favorite restaurant, favorite book/movie, or favorite music is not enjoyed by everyone else in your community. The music ministry in a church is an excellent example of what might attract or turn some people away from a church. Even the very best choir, contemporary band, or handbell group will not be to everyone's taste.

- What are people in our community looking for? How are they different from people in other communities? Think about the issues, hurts and challenges, as well as the strengths, the joys, and the celebrations of your community. Do not just assume you know your community. Get out and talk to some leaders, do some research, run a few MissionInsite (and/or other demographic) reports and learn about the people God calls you to serve and reach. There are examples of churches all over the country that have seen a need in their community and felt called to address that need. Examples include ministries like Celebrate Recovery, services for special needs children and their families, work reentry programs, grief counseling, etc. The answers to these questions will not give you your church's core values, but they will help to influence your discernment. An investment of time and energy to learn more about these areas will pay off in more clarity as you listen to God's Spirit.

- What is the history of the local community around your church? Why was this community founded? What have been the milestone events in the community? Do some research into the history of the area around your ministry. Even if you have lived there your whole life, you may be surprised at what you discover. There are many places around our country where things have changed so fast over the last few decades that those who live there now only have a "lifetime" memory. This is when a generation or two of people only view history as what has happened since they were born. This is a common trap we fall into when we fail to really understand the history of our mission field.

Imagine a new couple started attending

your church. They came to worship each weekend, got involved in serving, attended classes, were there for all the fellowship activities, and even became part of a committee or two. In other words, they jumped right in and did everything possible on the church's calendar. After a month or so, you went up to them and asked them to describe your church. While they might not use the word "values," the words and phrases they used would be great clues to the actual core values of your church. For example, they might talk about how they love serving in the food pantry, the message two weeks ago with a testimony from someone in the community whose bills the church helped pay, and a recent budget discussion at a meeting where more funds were allocated serving the homeless. In your mind, all of that would speak to the church's core value of Outreach. The connection between core values and the church's actions and behaviors may not always be that clear. However, the connection should always be in place.

Here is another way to look at core values. In this country, we have laws that we are expected to follow and not break. United Methodist churches (where I attend and serve as a judicatory leader) are expected to abide by the Book of Discipline for our denomination. While most churches would never consider breaking any laws or intentionally going against the *Book of Discipline,* they are also guided by their core values – even if they have never taken the time to identify those core values.

Three analogies might be helpful for you to think about and consider in your understanding of core values. Like most analogies, none of these are perfect, but they can be beneficial if the concept of core values is new.

The first analogy for core values is a guard rail on a road. If you have ever driven through the Appalachian Mountains, you have seen a lot of guard rails. These guard rails are in place to protect people in vehicles that go too far off the road from harm. You can see the evidence on many guard rails where they have been effective in doing so (dents, paint markings, etc.). While it might be expensive for someone to have their vehicle repaired from hitting a guard rail, it is, of course, better than injury or even death. Like guard rails on a road, core values in a local church can keep the ministry from harm by forming a protective barrier. The core values keep a church on the right road and out of trouble. Drivers on a road usually do not look at the guard rails. They keep their eyes on the road. But they are aware on some level that the guard rails are in place. Leaders in a church may not focus much on their core values. They are keeping their eyes on making disciples of Jesus Christ. However, they should be aware of core values in the ministry to guide them on how the church goes about making disciples of Jesus Christ.

The second analogy for core values is the banks of a river. Imagine a river flowing from a small stream up in the mountains into a strong river large enough for fishing, rafting, and even transporting boats at some stages. When most people picture a river, we tend to think more of the water and not as much of the banks. However, the banks of the river are what influence the river's direction and speed. This can be very true for the core values of a church, too. The core values may not be what most of us think of or encounter in an obvious way, but they will undoubtedly influence the ministry's direction and speed. Going back to the river for a moment, imagine there is a powerful rainstorm up in the mountains and that stream that flows into the river floods. The water is heading downstream much higher and faster than usual. The strength of the riverbanks will often determine whether or not the river will be able to handle the flood. This, too, can be true of the core values in a local church. All churches face a season or more of crisis during their lives. The ability of the church's leaders to weather that season of crisis will be influenced by the church's core values and the leaders' attention to those values. The core values may or may not prevent a crisis, but they can certainly increase the ministry's chances of weathering the storm.

The third analogy for core values is the boundaries of a soccer field. Go on Google and search "soccer pitch" or "football pitch," and you will see images for the playing surface for the game of soccer/football. Notice the outer boundaries, which form a rectangular shape around the perimeter of the field. When the game is being played, the ball must stay within that boundary. If the ball goes over the line, the play stops, and the other team takes possession. In most games, this does not happen very often. The players are aware of the boundaries, but that is not their focus. Even spectators watching the game know the boundaries are there, but their attention is usually on the players and the action happening on the field.

Church ministries also have boundaries. Pastors and church leaders do not talk about the boundaries very much, but they are always there. Boundaries such as:

- Federal, state, and local laws

- *The Book of Discipline,* if the church is United Methodist

- Any policies and procedures that the church may have created

- Customs, traditions, and unwritten rules within the church

- Core values

The object in the game of soccer is to score a goal. As long as the ball stays in the field of play, not going outside the boundaries, it is not helpful for the coach to try and dictate the exact movement of the ball from player to player. The coach will certainly create plays. The team will practice certain situations. But during the heat of the game, it becomes more about instincts, experience, and an overall understanding of the game for the players to score and win. A player who focuses too much on not breaking the rules and not kicking the ball out of bounds will often find themselves frozen with other players passing them by on the way to the goal.

In ministry, our goals are connected to Scripture. Our overall goal, also known as our mission, is to make disciples of Jesus. We find this clearly stated in the book of Matthew:

> *Jesus came near and spoke to them, "I've received all authority in heaven and on earth. Therefore, go and make disciples of all nations, baptizing them in the name of the Father and of the Son and of the Holy Spirit, teaching them to obey everything that I've commanded you. Look, I myself will be with you every day until the end of this present age."*

Matthew 28:18-20 (CEB)

Another goal in ministry, especially for those of us in leadership, is found in the book of Ephesians:

> *His purpose was to equip God's people for the work of serving and building up the body of Christ until we all reach the unity of faith and knowledge of God's Son. God's goal is for us to become mature adults – to be fully grown, measured by the standard of the fullness of Christ.*
>
> **Ephesians 4:12-1 (CEB)**

Those are two of the main goals of any church's ministry: make disciples and equip people for the work of God's Kingdom. We should not knowingly break the law as we are doing those: God's law or man's law. We should not knowingly violate any of our rules or policies. The core values we have in place will be there to guide us and keep us from trouble. But our main focus should be on scoring more goals, making disciples, and equipping people for the work of God's Kingdom. When a church, or ministry, or leader is too focused on the boundaries, they tend to forget our mission and our goals.

Have you ever seen a World Cup game where a home country's team scores a goal?

The crowd goes wild.

(Do a Google search for "World Cup announcer
Andres Cantor" to see a video and hear his
famous, "GGGOOOAAALLLLLL!!")

Imagine the reaction in your church if you
were to celebrate baptisms, confirmation classes,
or other signs of people growing closer to Christ
on their Spiritual journey the same way.

As stated before, none of these analogies
are perfect. Core values are not exactly like
the boundaries on a soccer/football pitch, or
exactly like the banks of a river, or exactly
like guard rails on a mountain road. However,
these analogies might help us understand the
overall concept of core values and their part in
our local church ministry.

In some cases, a pastor or laity leader
may find themselves way out in front of the
congregation. Their passion and drive for
ministry are such that they feel there is no time
to get to know the people in the congregation
or the community they are called to serve.
These leaders often have great intentions of
moving the church forward, but they find
themselves trying to do it all. Using the

analogy of the guard rail, one might say this described leader has unknowingly gone off the rails, unintentionally endangering the church's ministry. Spending time discerning the core values of a church is an investment of time and energy that will pay dividends for years to come. Likewise, investing time in understanding the core values of the expedition will pay dividends for years to come for the Expedition Team and the resulting ministry.

There are three basic approaches to discerning the core values for your church.

CHAPTER FOUR
Discerning the Core Values

*Then God came and stood before him exactly
as before, calling out, "Samuel! Samuel!"
Samuel answered, "Speak. I'm your servant,
ready to listen.*

1 Samuel 3:10 (MSG)

We will look at each of the three. As
we do so, think about any experiences you
have had in identifying core values at other
organizations.

The first way to identify the core values
of your church is just to name them. This
approach could be called "Name Them and
Claim Them." In this approach, a senior leader
(or maybe a small group of leaders) simply
picks their favorite core values (or the ones
they feel are most appropriate or accurate
for their organization) from a list and then

announces them publicly to their employees, congregation, investors, or other types of constituents. Some version of this approach is the most popular way for organizational leaders, both business and church, to list core values. Coming up with the organization's values this way is usually very efficient in that it can be done generally in one day or less. However, there are often challenges or outright dangers with coming up with your core values this way. What challenges or risks come to your mind?

The seventh-largest company in America in 2001, based on the Fortune500 revenue listing, was Enron Corporation. By the end of that year, Enron had filed for bankruptcy due to an accounting scandal. If you are not familiar with this story, it might be helpful to do a quick Google search for the basics of what happened. The irony here is Enron's listing of core values: respect, integrity, communication, and excellence. In hindsight, we can see how those values were not guiding the decisions of company leaders or the overall direction of the organization. Identifying core values is important but allowing them to guide our decisions is key.

Consider a local church whose pastor comes up with a list of core values in isolation. One of the values on the list is hospitality. The pastor has the best intentions because they know how important hospitality is for their congregation to start reaching new people on Sunday and then shares the whole list. Many people in the congregation see the word "Hospitality" and come up with a definition that is more about their comfort and less about welcoming new people. New bulletins are printed with the core values listed on the back. A new family comes to the church for the first time. An usher gives them a bulletin, but when they find a seat in the back pew so they can step out if their child gets fussy, a member of the church tells them that pew is where the Jones always sit. So, they move to another pew. On the way home, they see the values listed on the back of the bulletin and have a good laugh when they come to "hospitality."

Yes, these two examples may be more extreme than most churches' or organizations' situations. However, as leaders in ministry, we need to pay attention to any potential disconnections between our stated core values and the actions and behaviors of our congregation. No church or ministry leader will be perfectly in line with all core values every day or every time. However, that is our goal. Our actions and behaviors should match how we say we are going to act and behave.

The second approach to discerning the core values of your church is to conduct some type of survey. The audience for this survey could be as small as a select group of leaders in the congregation, as large as the entire congregation, or something in-between. Here is a sample of what that survey might look like:

First Church Core Values Survey

Directions: Using the scale below, circle the number that best expresses to what extent the following values are important to our church (actual values, not aspirational). Work your way through the list quickly, going with your first impression.

1 = not important   2 = somewhat important

3 = important   4 = most important

Preaching – communicating God's Word to people:

| | 1 | 2 | 3 | 4 |

Family – people immediately related to one another:

| | 1 | 2 | 3 | 4 |

Community – caring about and helping others:

| | 1 | 2 | 3 | 4 |

Giving – providing a portion of our finances to support ministry:

| | 1 | 2 | 3 | 4 |

Prayer – communicating with God:

| | 1 | 2 | 3 | 4 |

Evangelism – telling others the Good News about Christ:

| | 1 | 2 | 3 | 4 |

Fellowship – relating to and enjoying one another:

| | 1 | 2 | 3 | 4 |

Tradition – the customary ways or the "tried and true"

| | 1 | 2 | 3 | 4 |

Status quo – a preference for the way things are now:

| | 1 | 2 | 3 | 4 |

Creativity – coming up with new ideas and ways of doing ministry:

| | 1 | 2 | 3 | 4 |

Note how this example survey is asking the congregation to identify actual values, not aspirational values. This is an important distinction. *Actual values* are those we have seen evidence of in our ministry. Each person in the congregation will have a different perspective and experience with the church, so one person may have evidence of a value, and another person may not.

Aspirational values are ones we may not have in place right now in our church, but we feel strongly that they should be a value for us to work on and grow into a core value. An excellent example of this in some churches is evangelism. A congregation may feel that reaching new people and telling them the Good News of Jesus is very important. However, there is no objective evidence of this being done. The average attendance may have declined for years, and no one can recall the last time a first-time guest attended a worship service at the invitation of a member.

Choosing an aspirational value or two is acceptable in most situations. The church leaders just need to be very clear with everyone that the value is not currently in place but that they will be working with the congregation to ensure the presence of the value. Care should be taken not to unintentionally create a disconnect by communicating an aspirational value already in place. Likewise, there needs to be intentional decision-making and implementation to grow into making the aspirational core value a reality core value.

A large church in the St. Louis area surveyed the congregation a few years ago to identify their core values. The church had been using a list of core values for years to guide its ministry decisions and direction. Now they were undertaking a major strategic initiative and felt it was time to update the listing of core values. The pastors and leaders did an excellent job of teaching and communicating with the congregation about all aspects of their strategic initiative, including core values.

The online survey asked each person in the congregation to identify the top core values they saw currently in place in the church.

When the results came back, the pastors and leaders were a little surprised. The top two values identified by the congregation were "worship" and "music." After some time of reflection, the leaders realized what had happened. Because the church reached many unchurched people in the area, most of the people who completed the survey were not members of the church and mainly connected with the church during a worship service. So even though "worship" and "music" were not really top values in the church, they were the most visible expressions of ministry to those in the congregation who were only marginally connected to the church. Thus, they saw them as core values.

From the perspective of the pastors and leaders, evangelism was a core value. More specifically, the core value of evangelism focuses on reaching people who were not currently connected to a church. One expression of this core value and focus was expressed in the style of worship. So, the new people the church was reaching experienced passionate worship with outstanding music, cutting-edge technology, and pastors gifted in preaching. So those in the congregation naturally felt worship and music were core values of the church based on their experience. However, the pastors and leaders understood that what was really behind their worship services was the core value of evangelism. Both groups were correct. They were just viewing core values from a different perspective.

When a church like the one mentioned above embarks on a strategic ministry process, involving as much of the whole congregation as possible in some form of core values identification can be very beneficial. Many aspects of strategic ministry planning tend only to involve a small group of church leaders. So, finding a way to involve more of the overall congregation can help everyone feel like they had a voice and played a part in the whole process.

The third approach for discerning the core values for your church is a combination of the first two approaches with some intentional focus on discernment. Remember that the

information we are about to cover is not
intended as a checklist for you to complete
one task and then move to the next item. It is
provided as a guide for you to adapt to your
specific needs and to overlap areas when that
feels appropriate intentionally. Many of these
sections have been mentioned previously. The
intention now is to bring them all together
in a way you will be able to use. We will
walk through this approach in detail in the
following section.

CHAPTER FIVE
Core Value Discernment

Phase One: Prayer

Answer me when I cry out, my righteous God!
Set me free from my troubles!
Have mercy on me! Listen to my prayer!

Psalm 4:1 (CEB)

True discernment is not a formula or a structured process. Discernment is about positioning ourselves to hear the voice of the Holy Spirit best and understand how we are being guided. This phase of your expedition begins, ends, and is all about prayer.

Before you begin the process of discerning the core values for your church, spend time communicating with God through prayer – especially listening. As stated earlier, this is also a time to be prayer walking your community. Just take a slow walk (in pairs) up and down the streets, saying a short prayer over everyone and everything God shows you. Spend most of your prayer walking time just listening. What is God's Spirit saying to you? Be sure to gather your whole team together after each prayer walking session to compare notes and share what you saw and heard. Take note of those words and phrases which seem to keep coming up. Hang on to all this information. It will become a piece of your total core values discernment.

You should also create a plan to ensure all phases are covered in prayer during the prayer phase. None of this process should be a secret. Be sure you are letting the church prayer team and prayer warriors know what you are working on and ask for their specific prayers concerning discernment, wisdom, guidance, and for the Holy Spirit to speak and for you to hear that voice above all the other noise around you.

This may be a good time for you and your team to read *The Circle Maker: Praying Circles*

Around Your Biggest Dreams and Greatest Fears
by Mark Batterson. If your Expedition Team
has not yet read the book, *Open Road: The
Adventure of a Breakthrough Prayer Initiative*
by Sue Nilson Kibbey, I would encourage you
to all pause this core values process now to
read that book before continuing the values
identification. You may also want to establish
prayer partners within your team for this
season. Spending time in prayer with a partner
is a beautiful way to grow closer together as
you also grow closer to God.

Phase Two: Research

> *Ignorant desire isn't good; rushing feet make
> mistakes.*
>
> **Proverbs 19:2 (CEB)**

No matter what you and your Expedition
Team's level of understanding and experience
with core values is, this is a time to go deeper
and strengthen your knowledge level. The first
place to do so is in the Bible. We have already
looked at the core values of the early church
in Jerusalem (Acts 2:41-47 – evangelism,
instruction, fellowship, worship, and service).

> **Remember, all churches are unique; there is no church anywhere exactly like your church.**

Now take a look at a few more leaders and/or situations in Scripture. Look for what core values were influencing their decisions and the directions of the people they were leading. Try to identify at least two or three values for each leader. Some leaders from the Old and New Testaments will come to mind right away: Moses, Abraham, Joshua, Paul, Jesus, Peter, etc. Choosing one or two of them is fine.

Challenge your team to also look at leaders like Deborah, Miriam, Mary, Ruth, Esther, Lydia, etc. You might also want to look at certain situations or stories described in the Bible and identify the values that influenced those in that story or situation. Seeing values at work with God's people in Scripture can help you understand the importance of values along with deepening your knowledge. This will aid you later when it comes time to share and communicate your values.

The second place to research core values

focuses on other churches. The good news is that a part of this research can be done using Google on your computer. Just type in "core values church," and you will likely get over 112,000,000 results. The bad news is that now the work begins.

As stated earlier, all churches have core values, but most have never done the hard work of identifying them. Another challenge is that the nature of core values makes them more of an internal thing, so even when a church has identified their core values, they may not have made them public in such a way that they show up on an internet search. Your goal here is to find at least three churches with identified core values where you can relate to both the church and their values.

Remember, all churches are unique; there is no church anywhere exactly like your church. However, all churches are also more alike than they are different. So, many churches out there will have a similar story, a relatable context, and values that you might see applicable in your ministry. Search out at least three of these types of churches. If they are in your denomination, that is a bonus.

Once you have identified those churches, contact the pastor at that church. Ask them if it would be possible for you to have a few minutes of their time to talk about their church's core values. Let them know this is part of the discernment process for your church as you identify the core values for your ministry.

Here are a few questions you might consider asking them:

- Please describe the process your church used in identifying your core values. (If they were not there during that time, ask them to share what they know. You might inquire if there is someone else there you can speak to who was involved in the process.)

- How were the core values communicated to the congregation?

- How are you currently using core values in your leadership decision-making and direction choosing process?

- What, if anything, would you do differently if you were starting the values discernment process now?

- What advice would you give us as we embark on this journey of values discernment?

During the research time of your core values discernment, you may also find it helpful to read a few books about strategic planning, and the role values play in that thinking and process. There is a listing of suggested titles at the back of this book.

The research part of your values discernment process is a perfect place to divide your team and ask them to take a smaller piece of the total. For example, you might ask two people to contact one of the churches you identified and two other people to contact another church. Doing a smaller piece together with another person is an excellent way to help them bond by completing a task. Be sure you plan a time for the whole team to come back together so you can hear what everyone learned during their research time. Processing the findings together is very important to the overall discernment.

Phase Three: Congregational Survey

From now on, brothers and sisters, if anything is excellent and if anything is admirable, focus your thoughts on these things: all that is true, all that is holy, all that is just, all that is pure, all that is lovely, and all that is worthy of praise.

Philippians 4:8

For churches that have identified their core values, conducting a congregational survey is a very common option. As we covered earlier, there are some important factors to consider when a church leadership team is approaching this phase. For example:

- Who is our audience? Are we going to survey the whole congregation or just some segment of that whole? In some churches, the members of the church and the whole congregation are the same. In other churches, those can be two very different groups.

- How are we going to administer the survey? Will it be online, or paper, or both? There are pluses and minuses to both online-only and paper-only. You will need to factor in the age of your congregation and their comfort/accessibility to using an online survey such as SurveyMonkey.

- What exactly are we asking the congregation to identify with this survey? Our current values as demonstrated by our actions and behaviors as a church? They think we should have the values as a church, even if they are not in place now (also known as aspirational values). Some combination? The instructions to the congregation, both written and spoken, are very important to ensure you receive the information you need in this core values discernment process.

- When are we going to conduct the congregational values survey? Your overall journey on this expedition is certainly a factor. However, you will also need to think about the time of year, major events/activities already planned for your church and other factors that may affect the response rate for your survey.

- What happens after the survey? Who will be responsible for tabulating the results? Do we need to see each survey or only focus on the totals? The size of your congregation may be a factor in answering these questions.

The following is a sample of a congregational core values survey. In this example, the church is asking the congregation to identify three things:

1. Values they feel the ministry is currently demonstrating consistently and are guiding the church's direction and decision-making process.

2. Values they feel the ministry is demonstrating, but not doing so consistently. These might be values the congregation sees in one area of ministry, but not in all areas. These might also be values that the church is currently growing out of or into.

3. Values they feel are not in place currently in the church but should be to become the church God is calling. These are aspirational values. In churches that are also working on or have recently completed a visioning process, a new or aspirational value can be needed to support new ministry direction.

Springfield Church
Core Values Survey

Instructions: Place an "X" in the appropriate column

- Choose up to five (5) values you feel our church demonstrates consistently and guides all that we do.

- Choose up to three (3) values you feel our church demonstrates, but not consistently.

- Choose up to two (2) values you feel are not in place currently in our church but should be for us to become the church God is calling us to be.

	Value	Consistent	Inconsistent	Aspirational
1	Fellowship – enjoying time with each other			
2	Prayer – communicating with God			
3	Excellence – doing our very best in all we do			
4	Servanthood – putting others first			
5	Worship – gathering to praise God			
6	Preaching – sharing God's Word			
7	Apply Scripture – putting God's Word into action			
8	Innovation – new ways to be more effective			
9	Tradition – honoring the past			
10	Compassion – caring for the well-being of others			
11	Leadership – growing the ability to influence			
12	Outreach – caring for those around us			
13	Missions – caring for those around the world			
14	Creativity – artistic ways to do ministry			
15	Discipleship – creating followers of Jesus			
16	Evangelism – telling others about Jesus			
17	Generosity – offering our money to God			
18	Encouragement – offering hope and support			
19	Diversity – embracing differences among us			

20	Mobilized – equipping everyone to help			
21	Bible – know and remember biblical truths			
22	Families – engaging multiple generations			
23	Integrity – doing what we say we will do			
24	Unchurched – attracting those who do not attend church			
25	Intentionality – planning for what we must do			
26	Obedience – following God and leaders			
27	Christian Groups – gathering to grow in faith			
28	Christ-Centered – ensuring all we do reflects Jesus			
29	Children & Youth – helping kids grow in faith			
30	Cooperation – working together to serve Jesus			
31	Risk-Taking – willing to try new things			
32	Relevance – understandable and applicable today			
33	Accountability – holding people responsible			
34	Growth – expand our reach and impact			
35	Authenticity – being ourselves always			
36	Fruitfulness – focus on results for God's Kingdom			
37	Joy – fun, laughter, and amusement			
38	Open-minded – able to consider other ideas and perspectives			

Remember, the previous survey was just an example. The values you list can and should be different. Your Expedition Team will need to consider your congregation, your context in the area, and all the other factors throughout this book when you come up with your master listing of values for the survey.

You will also need to create your definitions of each value. Without definitions, people will interpret the word differently, and therefore the results will not be accurate. The example above only uses a few words to describe each value. That may work well for your congregation, or you may need to include a more detailed description. You will also need to consider places where your definition of a value may differ from how you see it elsewhere.

Another thing to consider with the values survey is where there might be some confusion between two or more very similar values. For example, some people might use the words "outreach" and "missions" interchangeably. If you list them both on your survey, you will need to be sure the definitions clarify the difference.

For some people in the congregation, there may be a sense that we are asking them to rank or prioritize the values. Some people may not understand that even if the church does not choose "children and youth" as a value, we will still have that ministry, and the church will continue to focus on children and youth. In most cases, congregational values surveys contain so many positive attributes that it can be overwhelming for some people only to choose a few values. These are all reasons the church leaders need to be clear in the communication, and the congregation values survey instructions. Each person in the congregation will fill any perceived gap in communication or instructions - usually with something different from what you intended.

Best Practices

The following are best practices as you plan to conduct the congregation values survey. The Expedition Team will need to adapt to your church context:

- Preach on strategic ministry planning. Some churches may want to do a sermon series on topics such as core values, mission, vision, and setting goals. There are many examples throughout the Bible of each area, and the book of Nehemiah contains examples of each element and the overall process. You might consider opening the core values survey to the congregation the week you preach on that topic.

- Intentionally end the worship service 10 minutes early one Sunday and transition into the core values survey. This will give you an excellent opportunity to have a majority of your congregation in one place and available. With a minute or two of instructions, you could ask the ushers to pass out paper copies of the survey. If you are doing the survey online, you might have the link in the bulletin, on a screen, or in your church app. If you are doing both paper and online, this is a perfect opportunity to involve everyone there that day in worship. The people doing the survey online can be doing that simultaneously as the people completing the survey on paper. Don't forget those who may be worshiping with you from home or who might watch your service later online. Be sure to include a way for them to either get a paper copy of the survey or provide a link to the online version.

- Plan on keeping the survey open for two to four weeks. Most churches will need to spend at least two weekends talking about the values survey to reach a majority of the congregation. The first weekend might be the time you preach on values, end a little early, and ask people to complete the survey before they leave. The second weekend you may want to announce the survey to those who may not have been there the previous weekend, have copies available if you are doing paper surveys, and plan on having someone available to answer questions. Depending on your church, you may want to repeat this another weekend or two.

- Have a set date where the survey will no longer be open. No matter what size your church, or the amount of effort you put into getting people to complete the core values survey, you will never get one hundred percent of your congregation. A good target might be to receive surveys back from seventy percent of the households who regularly attend your church services.

- Thank people for taking the time to complete the survey. Let them know that this is just one phase in the overall core values discernment process. Inform them that the survey results will be shared with appropriate church leaders, and they will hear more about the church's core values in a few weeks. Caution should be used when sharing anything more than that with the overall congregation. The survey is not intended to be a way for people to "vote" for their favorite values or areas of ministry. Publishing the actual results from the survey could lead to some uncomfortable situations where it might appear there are "winners" and "losers," or someone sees where they were the only person to indicate a certain value. The congregational values survey is intended to be a piece of the process but not the whole process.

Phase Four: Church Leadership

Without guidance, a people will fall, but there is victory with many counselors."

Proverbs 11:14 (CEB)

The overall size of your church will influence this phase, your number of ministry leaders (paid and unpaid), and how many, if any, of the church leaders are a part of the Expedition Team on this journey. For example, you may be in a situation where your whole leadership team is on the Expedition Team due to your church size or maybe the fact that your church is brand new and just getting started. To explain this phase of the core values discernment process, we will assume you are a church that has been in place for many years, and some, but not all, of your church leaders are on the Expedition Team. Please adjust what is covered below to your specific situation.

In this phase, your focus is on the church leaders. In some cases, all or some of these leaders may be part of the church's paid staff. You are encouraged to think of church leaders in the broadest possible way for this phase. Consider your response to this question, "Who are the people in our church who have the greatest influence on the congregation?" In many churches, the answer to that question will include some people who do not hold any official role or position within the church. Come up with as complete a listing as possible for your church leaders.

The leaders you identify should be instructed not to complete the congregation's core values survey unless they cannot participate in this leadership phase. A spouse or other member of the immediate family completing the survey is okay. You just want to avoid as much duplication as possible.

Invite the leaders to gather one afternoon or evening for a time of prayer, discussion, and discernment of the church's core values. Prior to the time together, provide them with an overview of the whole core values discernment process, a listing of values you are considering along with definitions of each value, and an agenda for the gathering. A best practice would be to ask them to read and spend some time in prayer over Acts chapter two.

The purpose of this gathering is not for the church leaders to just complete the same values survey as the congregation. It is a time for them to discuss the values and come to a consensus on a few using prayer and discernment.

- After an opening time of prayer and devotion on Acts chapter two verses 41-47, divide the overall group into smaller groups of no more than six people. Pass out copies of the values, including the descriptions of each, to all of the smaller teams. Give each team/table a large flip chart page with markers.

- Set some ground rules for this leadership gathering such as all voices are important, everyone should be given a chance to speak; we need to hear from everyone in the room, you may be the one God is speaking through during our gathering; the time for discussion is now, we will not leave something unsaid here only to speak it somewhere else; our personal agenda and preferences need to be left at the door so that we can discern what is best for our total ministry. This can be challenging when a leader is very involved, and obviously passionate, about a specific ministry. (Children, youth, music, outreach, recovery, etc.) Encourage all the leaders to remove their specific ministry area hat for a while, and to put on the total church hat as much as possible. Experience has shown that the group may need to be reminded about this several times during the session.

- Instruct the teams that they will have twenty minutes to discuss the values and agree on the two values they feel are most consistently in place and being practiced now in the church. (This should be enough time if all the leaders have seen the values listing and descriptions before this gathering.)

- Bring the whole group back together and hear from each team/table the two values they feel are most consistently in place now in the church. Encourage everyone to ask questions where they need more information.

- Pause the process long enough to pray for the Holy Spirit to guide your hearts, minds and give you the wisdom needed to discern God's will.

- Using consensus, determine which two values the total leadership group feels are most consistently in place now in the church. These are the values that most often guide the decisions the church makes. Do not just vote on the values. This will create "winners" and "losers" since no value will likely be a unanimous choice.

- Repeat this same basic process to identify one value the leadership group feels is in place in the church, but inconsistently, and one value the leadership group feels needs to be identified as an aspirational value for the church to move into where God is calling them.

- Pause for prayer and maybe a break or two when you feel the group needs it.

- End with a time of celebration. Thank everyone for their time, and be sure to explain to them the remaining phases in the core values discernment process.

Remember, the following was just an example for you to adjust as needed to your church situation. Now is a good time for you to look back over phases one to four and make notes about what these will look like for your church. What adjustments might you need to make? Who else in your church needs to be involved in some or all these phases? What does the timeline for these phases look like for your church?

Before we go to the next phase, let's talk about working with a coach. As you can tell, the core values discernment process will take some quality time and commitment from your team as you journey on the expedition. Working with a professional coach along the way will give you someone objective to bounce ideas off, discuss options for each phase, and encourage you when things do not go exactly as planned. You can learn more about working with a professional coach at:

- **Coaching4Clergy** (www.coaching4clergy.com)

- **International Coaching Federation**
  (www.coachfederation.org)

Phase Five: Assemble

Now finish the job as well so that you finish it with as much enthusiasm as you started, given what you can afford.

2 Corinthians 8:11 (CEB)

Completing the previous four phases will give you everything you need to complete the process of discerning the core values for your church. This phase is all about bringing all that information together, so you and your team can best discern those values. Schedule a time for your whole team to gather to complete this phase. Plan for adequate time so the team can process the information, ask questions, and finally discern the final listing of core values for your church.

Go back now and review the work you completed in each of those four phases. Think of each phase as being pieces of a puzzle. No one phase will give you all the pieces you need to complete the whole puzzle. Some phases may fill in more or less of the puzzle than others, but all are required to give you the complete picture. Using a whiteboard, flip chart page, or another tool, divide the available space into four sections. For example:

Prayer	Research
Congregation Survey	Church Leadership

In the prayer phase: What did you hear from the Holy Spirit as you were prayer walking around the church? What values, words, phrases, or images stand out from your time in prayer? Write down the words or phrases in the appropriate space on your chart. If an image is important in this stage, then draw it in the same space.

In the research phase: What did you learn from reading and studying leaders in the

Bible? Besides Acts 2:41-47, what other values stood out to you from your scripture readings? What did you learn from talking with pastors and leaders at other churches about their experiences concerning core values? What words, phrases, or images stand out from your time in research? Write down the words or phrases in the appropriate space on your chart. If an image is important in this stage, then draw it in the same space.

In the congregation survey phase: Which five values did the congregation feel were consistently demonstrated in our church? Which three values did the congregation feel were being demonstrated, but not consistently, in our church? Which two values did the congregation feel were not in place currently in our church, but should be for us to become the church God is calling us to be? Write down each of your responses in the appropriate space on your chart. Be sure it is clear which ones are consistent, inconsistent, and aspirational.

In the church leadership phase: Which two values did the church leadership feel are consistently demonstrated in our church?

Which one value did the church leadership feel was being demonstrated, but not consistently, in our church? Which one value did the church leadership feel was not in place currently in our church, but should be for us to become the church God is calling us to be? Write down each of your responses in the appropriate space on your chart. Be sure it is clear which ones are consistent, inconsistent, and aspirational.

This may be the first time your Expedition Team has seen all of this information presented in one place. You may want to pause for a time of prayer before you go any further. Allow time for people to process the information before moving into questions, comments, or any form of decision-making.

Once the team is ready, go around the group and give each person an opportunity to ask questions or comment on anything they see on the chart. Keep everyone focused on the task at hand and avoid any conversation which may be critical or negative about anyone on the team, in the congregation, or in any particular phase. Encourage each person to add something to the discussion based on what they see on the chart and feel God's Spirit might be saying to them.

Most likely, you and the team are now able to see a trend in the information on the chart. Several values have likely risen to the top and are standing out above the rest. You may also have some clarity on an aspirational value.

There is no perfect number of values for a church to use. However, five or six core values are most common. Some churches will expand this by listing two values together like "Worship & Preaching" or "Excellence & Creativity." Narrow the list down until it feels appropriate without being overwhelming. Use the same process as the church leadership phase if that will help finding consensus. As in the church leadership phase, avoid just voting on all the values. Keep the aspirational values in mind, too. Most churches would not find it helpful to have more than one or two aspirational values, but there may be one on that list the team feels needs to be included.

This part of your gathering will take as long as it takes. Be careful trying to rush the discernment process. A good practice is to pause for prayer after you add each value to your final list. This is an excellent way to clear your mind before you discuss and discern the next value.

A word of caution: it is rare, but in some cases, what is presented as a value is shown in a negative form and not in a positive form. For example, "serving those the city and others are ignoring." Care should be used not to leave any of your final core values words, phrases, or descriptions in any type of negative form. Core values should be listed positively.

Imagine a church communicating, even internally only, against the seven deadly sins:

- Pride

- Greed

- Lust

- Envy

- Gluttony

- Anger

- Sloth

While that might be true, it still comes across as negative instead of positive. That church might be better served by saying they are in favor of the Fruits of the Spirit (from Galatians 5:22):

- Love

- Joy

- Peace

- Patience

- Kindness

- Generosity

- Faithfulness

- Self-control

After this gathering, your team should have the final listing of core values for your church. While this is not "the end," it is a great place to stop and celebrate. You may want to plan for some type of team celebration. This is also a perfect time to end a gathering with communion.

Phase Six: Communicate

Pleasant words are flowing honey, sweet to the taste, and healing to the bones.

Proverbs 16:24 (CEB)

Once you have the final listing of core values for the church, they will need to be communicated to everyone. Remember to use the definitions of the core values rather than just the words in your communication to ensure clear understanding and messaging. Do not wait to work on your communication strategy until the final core values list has been identified. Start planning out the communication of the values from the beginning of this discernment process.

Core values are different from other areas of your strategic ministry planning process. For example, the mission of a church is usually very public. You will find a church's mission statement on their website, social media, worship service bulletin, newsletters, etc. Some churches will even have the mission statement painted on a wall for everyone to see. Core values are more internal than external. Not that they need to be a secret, they just tend to be mainly used by church leaders to make decisions and guide ministry direction. So, as you think about your communication strategy for the new core values, your focus will likely be internal.

Treat this like the big deal that it is. You have discerned the core values God wants your church leaders to use as they guide the ministry into God's vision for your future! That is a major accomplishment. To repeat what was covered earlier, all churches have core values. Most have just never taken the time to identify them. Your church is now in a small percentage of churches that understand the power of using core values to guide your decisions and direction. Some events and activities in the church are appropriately communicated in the worship bulletin, an announcement from the pulpit, or in the church newsletter, etc. Sharing the new core values might call for more of an "Announcement Party" type celebration. Some churches have gone as far as having items made with their core values printed on them for people to take home and remember the values (mugs, water bottles, mouse pads, phone cases, notebooks, etc.).

As you prepare to communicate the new core values to your church, consider sharing them first with the church leaders from phase four. These church leaders are the ones who will be using the core values the most in decision-making and ministry directions. By communicating the new core values list to them first, you honor their leadership and give them time to process and ask questions before communicating to the rest of the church. You are not going to them for approval. You are just sharing with them first. (Voting on or asking to approve something we have done through discernment is not God-honoring. Be sure this is clear to everyone very early in this overall process so you can avoid any misunderstandings later.) Thank all of the church leaders for their part in the whole discernment process. Help them to see how the final listing was created.

These church leaders can be great advocates as you continue the communication strategy. The communication to the church leaders and the communication to the rest of the church should occur as close in time as possible. You do not want to put people in a position where they are being asked to keep anything secret for long.

The communication strategy will also need to include the exact word or phrase used for each core value, the description of each core value, and at least one Bible verse that can be shared with each core value. While most surveys and many listings of values focus on just one word, you may find it more helpful to use a few words or even a short phrase. Some churches will communicate their core values in a full sentence, but this is rare. Most core values for a church can be communicated in a word or a few words. Looking back to the survey, you will see examples of concise descriptions for each value.

Your final listing of core values may be better served with a complete sentence or two of description. When you communicate this final list, it is important to be clear about your meaning for each value. This is where a clear and complete description can be beneficial.

If people are confused or uncertain about

any values, they will likely come up with their definition. Chances are good their definition will be different than yours. Adding a scripture verse to each core value will also help communicate the connection between the value and what the Bible says about the value or an example of where that value is shown in the Bible.

The following is an example of what this would look like for a team to communicate the core value of worship to their leaders and congregation:

Worship

We value worship as fundamental to the life of faith and an authentic expression of praise to God and God's grace through Jesus Christ. Worship includes our gathering together in celebration at our weekly worship service but should permeate all our church is and does.

Worship the Lord your God,
and serve him only.

Matthew 4:10

Let everything that has breath praise
the Lord, praise the Lord.

Psalm 150:6

Expressions of worship include, but are not limited to: preaching, music, prayer, offering, fellowship, and the celebration of the sacraments (communion and baptism). We value the plethora of creative ways in which we can participate and share the good news of Jesus Christ in a lifestyle of worship.

**Morning Star Church, a United Methodist congregation
in Darden Prairie, Missouri, 2015**

Even if your church also ended up with the core value of "worship" on your final listing, your definition can and should be different. The definitions you use, the Bible verses, and the words and phrases you use for your core values need to be chosen for your church.

This following example is from the business world. Local churches do not have the same resources as multi-billion-dollar businesses, but there are always things we can learn to adapt to our context and situation.

In 2003 Boise Cascade Corporation acquired OfficeMax, and the company changed its name officially to OfficeMax. This was the merger of two huge organizations. Like most mergers, the financial areas tend to get the most attention, but the combining of cultures determines whether a merger will ultimately work. (By the way, this is also true in the church world.) The Chief Executive Officer of the organization and the Board of Directors spent time coming up with new values. They then partnered with the company's marketing and training divisions to create a strategy for sharing those values with everyone in the new organization. This strategy included basic training on the definitions and importance of mission, vision, and values. The new values were: integrity & accountability; think company & customer first; teamwork & trust; focus & discipline; sense of urgency. A main image was created of a sailboat, with the sails representing the values, the wind in the sails was the mission, and the sailboat was moving toward the company vision.

Culture is the most potent force in any organization, church, or business. Core values and culture tend to be the unseen forces that influence, guide, shape all aspects of leadership decisions, ministry direction, and much more throughout your church. Investing the time to discern your core values, give them a name, and intentionally communicate them to your congregation makes them real and almost tangible. It shines a light on your values and helps everyone to see them clearly.

One church went through the process of discerning its core values as part of strategic ministry planning work. They then had someone paint the words they used for their values on the room walls the church used for leadership meetings. The values were painted on the top border section of all four walls, so every time leaders met in that room, their values were surrounding them on the walls. Those values were there to remind them and to guide them. The values borders gave them a visual reminder of something which too many organizations lose sight of once the values survey is completed.

Painting a values border on the meeting room might not be appropriate for your church. However, you should think about how you can keep the new core values in front of your church leaders and not let this discernment process turn into a one-time task when the whirlwind of ministry changes your focus.

Hopefully, you are reading this book prior to embarking on the core values portion of your expedition. If so, now is a good time to identify who on your team will be responsible for the communication strategy. They should not try to do this all on their own, but it is good for someone on your Expedition Team to be the point person for communications. As you are creating your timeline for discerning the new core values for your church, be sure this communications strategy is well represented, and you are working together with the appropriate people elsewhere in your church.

Phase Seven: Live Into

Don't remember the prior things; don't ponder ancient history. Look! I'm doing a new thing; now it sprouts up; don't you recognize it? I'm making a way in the desert, paths in the wilderness.

Isaiah 43:18, CEB

You have completed all the previous phases. You have discerned the church's core values and have clearly communicated them to the leaders and the whole congregation. Now you can just sit back and watch them work their magic. Sorry to burst your bubble. All of the previous phases are, of course important. Yes, if you have intentionally discerned your core values, you are in a very small group of churches. However, just having identified core values is not the point. Remember the example of Enron Corporation from earlier? That may be an extreme example, but just having core values will not do anything for your ministry. The real work comes from intentionally using them to guide your leadership decisions and ministry direction.

Throughout this book, we have talked about how core values guide leadership decisions and ministry direction. Now is the time for us to unpack that concept. Think about all of the leadership meetings you have attended over the years at a church. What were the most common topics on the agenda? Most church leadership meetings focus on finances, facilities, and fires. Do we have enough money to pay our bills? How are the buildings and grounds holding up? What crisis do we need to address right now? That may be an oversimplification, but it is probably very close. As your leadership team begins to move into a place where more time is spent on where God is calling the ministry (vision) and the goals you set to get there, the use of core values to guide your decisions becomes critical. Church leaders must be accountable to the core values of the ministry.

- How would you define the word "accountability?"

- What has been your experience with accountability outside the local church?

- What has been your experience with accountability in a local church?

- Where have you seen accountability modeled positively?

Accountability should not be defined as a punitive response to something going wrong. Accountability means preventing something from going wrong.

Henry J. Evans

In our culture today, accountability is most often seen as negative or punitive. Too often, accountability shows up when something goes wrong, and people are looking to lay blame. The finger-pointing begins.

In reality, achieving our mission, honoring our core values, moving into God's vision for our church begin with accountability. Accountability can and should be positive in a church. Consider the example of a small group of believers doing life together in some form of Christian community (Celebrate Recovery, Sunday school class, small group, etc.). One person in the group might share something they are struggling with and ask the others to hold them accountable in their meetings.

"Mary, you told us last week that you wanted to read a chapter from the Bible each night before bedtime. How are you doing with that?"

Positive accountability. Accountability is born when two or more people know about a commitment. Discerning the church's core values and asking the leaders to use those values as they make decisions is a commitment. Some churches may want to incorporate their core values and the commitment to guide decisions into some form of leadership covenant. In accountable cultures in a local church, everyone holds each other accountable for their commitments positively and productively.

Church leaders are making decisions all the time. In some cases, those are small decisions like, "Should we renew our copier contract?"

Other times the decisions are major ones that will potentially impact the ministry direction of the church for years. "Is it time to add another worship service?" or "Should we purchase the property next door so we can expand our parking lot?" or maybe, "Is God calling us to grow by starting another campus?"

The mission and vision of the church will be factors in those major leadership decisions. The core values will also guide and influence the leaders. Imagine one of your church's core values is encouragement. You define it as:

- Encouragement: We desire to give hope to people who need hope:

And let us consider how we may spur one another toward love and good deeds. Let us not give up meeting together, as some are in the habit of doing, but let us encourage one another – and all the more as you see the Day approaching.

Hebrews 10:24-25 (NIV)

During a leadership meeting at your church, it is announced that the property next door is finally going up for sale. Your church has been wanting to purchase that property for years. A discussion starts about how the church should use the property if they can buy it. One leader mentions the core value of encouragement and suggests that the home be converted into a shelter for women transitioning from abusive relationships. Another leader suggests tearing down the old house on the property so the church can expand its parking lot to make room for more people to attend worship services. This second leader points to the Scripture used for the encouragement value to support their suggestion.

A passionate discussion begins involving all the church leaders. After prayer and discernment, the leadership team decides to move forward with the first option. As much as they need more parking for worship, the women's shelter ministry seems like a clearer expression of their core value of encouragement. This is an example of a core value in action.

For your core values to really be in place at your church, they need to be expressed in tangible ways. People need to see them in action. Members and leaders in your congregation should be able to point to activities, events, actions connected to your church and say, "There, that is our core value of _____ in action!"

One way to see if this is happening in your church is to take your listing of core values and place it alongside your church calendar. Try to identify items on the calendar that will connect to each of your core values. Pay special attention not just to the words or your core values but also to their descriptions.

For example, your church may have the core value of "Worship," and you point to the weekend services on the calendar as a clear connection to that value. While that may be true, look at what you wrote for the description of the worship value. The connection might be there, but it also may have some room to grow.

If you are not careful, an aspirational value you identified might never make it onto the church calendar. It is easier for us to keep doing what we have always done than to intentionally move a church into aligning our actions to our values.

For your church's core values to truly guide the leadership decisions and ministry direction of the church, they need to be visible and intentionally revisited often. This does not mean going back through all the phases we outlined in this book every year. The core values you identified for your church will likely stay the same for many years. These are the foundation of your ministry. That foundation will not change unless there is a significant shift in your ministry. Revisiting your core values might mean planning an annual leadership retreat where the church's core values are shared again as part of any new strategic ministry plans or leadership development initiatives.

Revisiting the core values might also include printing them on the leadership meeting agenda and taking time during each session to discuss one of the values and share examples of that value in action. The book, Strategy Matters: Your Roadmap for an Effective Ministry Planning Retreat by Kay Kotan and Ken Willard would be a good resource to use. The key is to be intentional about keeping your core values alive and to use these values as guides for your decisions and direction. May God bless you and your Expedition Team on this journey!

Additional Resources

Additional books to learn more about core values and strategic ministry planning:

Strategy Matters: Your Roadmap for an Effective Ministry Planning Retreat
by Kay Kotan and Ken Willard

Advanced Strategic Planning: A New Model for Church and Ministry Leaders
by Aubrey Malphurs

Church Unique: How Missional Leaders Cast Vision, Capture Culture, and Create Movement
by Will Mancini

Leading Congregational Change: A Practical Guide for the Transformational Journey
by Jim Herrington, Mike Bonem, and James H. Furr

Strategic Thinking: How to Sustain Effective Ministry
by Thomas G. Bandy

From Values to Action: The Four Principles of Values-Based Leadership
by Harry M. Jansen Kraemer Jr.

Acknowledgments

All of us working in the church world today stand on the shoulders of those who came before us. There are countless church consultants, authors, leaders and friends who I've had the privilege and honor to work alongside and learn from over the years. People such as:

- George Bullard
- Aubrey Malphurs
- Bob Farr
- Kay Kotan
- David Hyatt
- John Ewart
- Paul Borden
- Gary McIntosh
- Lyle Schaller
- Bill Easum
- Bob Whitesel
- Thom Rainer
- Jim Barber
- and many others

I would like to thank everyone who has helped me on this journey to equip God's people to expand God's Kingdom.

Quotes From Other Books
in The Greatest Expedition Series

The multi-site movement keeps the church centered on God's consistent call to go and make disciples for the transformation of the world while staying connected to one another in community.

Ken Nash
Multi-Site Ministry

Stay flexible even when it is not easy. Due to the stress and responsibility of ministry, we can become rigid, pessimistic and fail to see the opportunities in front of us. A mark of great leadership is flexibility, being able to make adjustments when necessary.

Olu Brown
New Kind of Venture Leader

But let me be clear, we will not be making the case that online relationships and connections are the same as in-person ones; we all know they are not. But we will be talking about why online connections are valuable, and there is nothing "virtual" or "almost" about them.

Nicole Reilley
Digital Ministry

Quotes From Other Books
in The Greatest Expedition Series

While we find struggling churches in different contexts, theological backgrounds, sizes, and cultures, declining congregations have one thing in common: There is a palpable lack of focus on what God desires.

Jaye Johnson
Missional Accountability

How you think of your church will determine not only your priorities, but also your energy investment and actions. It will define how you lead and to what extent you live into what the church of Jesus Christ is intended to be.

Sue Nilson Kibbey
Open Road

Any collaboration with local people is a good thing – but the best collaboration is spiritual. It is where we begin to pray together about the community, and the emerging ministry. In such a spiritual collaboration, amazing things begin to happen.

Paul Nixon
Cultural Competency

What is *The Greatest Expedition*?

The Greatest Expedition is a congregational journey for churches, charges, or cooperative parishes led by a church Expedition Team of 8-12 brave pioneering leaders. The purpose of *The Greatest Expedition* is to provide an experience for Expedition Teams to explore their local context in new ways to develop new MAPS (ministry action plans) so you are more relevant and contextual to reach new people in your community. Updated tools and guides are provided for the church's Expedition Team. Yet, it is a "choose your own adventure" type of journey.

The tools and guides will be provided, but it is up to the church's Expedition Team to decide which tools are needed, which tools just need sharpening, which tools can stay in their backpack to use at a later time, what pathways to explore, and what pathways to pass.

the greatest
EXPEDITION

The Greatest Expedition provides a new lens and updated tools to help your Expedition Team explore and think about being the church in different ways. Will your Expedition Team need to clear the overgrown brush from a once known trail, but not recently traveled? Or will the Expedition Team need to cut a brand new trail with their new tools? Or perhaps, will the Team decide they need to move to a completely fresh terrain and begin breaking ground for something brand new in a foreign climate?

Registration is open and Expedition Teams are launching!

greatestexpedition.com

the greatest
EXPEDITION

A New Kind
of
**Venture
Leader**

Olu Brown

EXPANDING
THE
EXPEDITION
THROUGH

**Digital
Ministry**

Nicole Reilley

the greatest
EXPEDITION

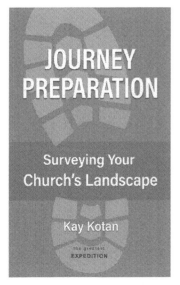

**JOURNEY
PREPARATION**

Surveying Your
Church's Landscape

Kay Kotan

the greatest
EXPEDITION

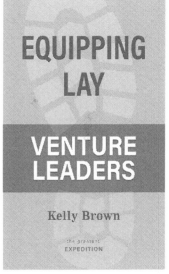

**EQUIPPING
LAY**

**VENTURE
LEADERS**

Kelly Brown

the greatest
EXPEDITION

MarketSquareBooks.com

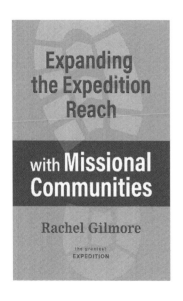

Expanding
the Expedition
Reach

with **Missional
Communities**

Rachel Gilmore

the greatest
EXPEDITION

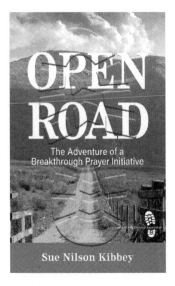

OPEN
ROAD

The Adventure of a
Breakthrough Prayer Initiative

Sue Nilson Kibbey

**MULTI-SITE
MINISTRY**

expanding the
Expedition Reach

KEN NASH
with Kristen Farrell

the greatest
EXPEDITION

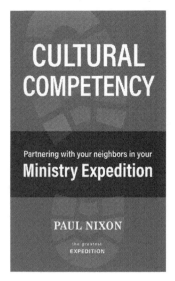

**CULTURAL
COMPETENCY**

Partnering with your neighbors in your
Ministry Expedition

PAUL NIXON

the greatest
EXPEDITION

MarketSquareBooks.com

MarketSquareBooks.com

KAY KOTAN & KEN WILLARD

STRATEGY MATTERS

YOUR ROADMAP FOR AN EFFECTIVE MINISTRY PLANNING RETREAT

OBJECTIVES

GOALS

VISION

MISSION

CORE VALUES

MarketSquareBooks.com

Church Ecology

Creating a
Leadership
Pathway
for Your
Church

Ken Willard & Kelly Brown

Introduction by Bishop Sandra Steiner Ball

MarketSquareBooks.com